CHOSEN

CHOSEN

Geoff Cochrane

Victoria University of Wellington Press

Victoria University of Wellington Press
PO Box 600, Wellington
New Zealand
vup.wgtn.ac.nz

A catalogue record is available from the
National Library of New Zealand.

ISBN 9781776564088

Printed in New Zealand by Ligare

CONTENTS

LONG AGO   9

A boy in a backyard   10

IN THE PONDS OF LOVELY MEAT   11

They're obviously students, yes   12

VERTIGO!   13

MUSIC AND SHOES   14

The Land of Cockaigne   15

JULY   16

BAD FOOT   17

NOT QUITE A MOONBOOT   18

AMBUSHING MYSELF   19

THE TATTOOED MAN   21

Coca-Cola   22

GOING TO THE PICTURES, WAY BACK
     WHEN   23

PENIS-ENVY *CIRCA* 1970   24

REMEMBERING JOHN'S SUICIDE BY
     SHOTGUN   25

KINGSBEER & CO   26

SUMMER   28

SOME QUESTIONS IT AMUSED ME TO
    ANSWER   31

SHOOT   32

GROWING UP IN TAMAR ST   34

MY FATHER'S TOOLS   35

LOSING MY WHISTLE   36

Sam's a smart young bloke . . .   37

CHOSEN   38

SUNDRIES   39

Ony in the quietest moments   40

THE SONG THRUSH AND ME   41

TALKING TO MYSELF (AGAIN)   42

IAN   43

IRRATIONALITY   44

ADDENDA   46

CHOSEN

LONG AGO

Morning's drenched grasses. Morning's grasses, drenched.

A boy in a backyard.
A boy in a backyard in Island Bay.
A boy in a backyard in Island Bay in 1958.

Whence and whither, Geoff?

IN THE PONDS OF LOVELY MEAT

6% of doctors still smoke.

*

Sane people living in a city
try to ensure that they never seem mad.

*

Richard Branson launched
his first business venture
from a phonebox.

*

'What size feet do you take?'

*

A consumer of medicines, that's me.
And last night I gave myself a shot
of the *wrong* insulin.

They're obviously students, yes,
and they're sitting side by side,
they're sitting side by side on the bus.

The smaller guy, the slender Asian kid,
looks somewhat upset and moist of eye,
but his senior-seeming friend
kisses him on the brow,
kisses him on the brow tenderly,
and the Kissed One reposes his head
on his comforter's shoulder.

VERTIGO!

Earlier this afternoon, my God,
an overwhelming dizziness beset me;
I had to stagger carefully
to the safety of a chair
and sit, appalled, until the spinning stopped,
until my gyros stabilized themselves.

And then, a sweaty nausea of fright.

And then, a craven loosening of bowels.

MUSIC AND SHOES

Volvo. Mazda. Alfa Romeo.
Fatties with their broken legs in casts.

*

A sprinkling of minims.
A spoonful of sprightly little crotchets.

*

Flies and bottletops.
Secular prayers.

(As a smoker, I'm always free
to have a cigarette; as a *non*-smoker,
I'd *nev*er be free to have one.)

*

I buy a pair of Lacoste sneakers
with wee green crocodiles on their sides.

Wee green crocodiles with red mouths.

Just saying.

The Land of Cockaigne.
A kind of paradise.
A place of clement friendships, quiet joys.
And I go there in my sleep,
I go there in my dreams;
I pop in for a drink from time to time.

JULY

Winter is already endless winter.
Deeply, sincerely winter.
But here he comes, an old guy wearing shades,
sunglasses of a black opacity.

BAD FOOT

My neighbour's tree has grown,
become more dense; no longer can I see
the red light on the hill.

*

I'm delaying, really.
Delaying's what I'm doing.
Delaying finding out
whether or not I've got
a broken bone in my foot.
(I rather think I have,
and I'd rather not know about it.)

*

I've been alive for aeons.
I've been alive for a very long time.

Trams of red and cream
ran through my childhood.
Island Bay was perfumed by burning leaves
(incinerators smoked in slow backyards),
and the city reeked of the sea
(Wellington was still a truly *maritime* concern).

NOT QUITE A MOONBOOT

He studies the X-rays and sees in them a fracture of the fourth metatarsal in my right foot, a stress fracture caused by my trying to break in a new pair of shoes.

Dr Tim Halpine, Doctor of Podiatric Medicine, DPM (USA) MPNZ. Thus reads his card, and his rooms on The Terrace are well-lit, their walls bedecked with family photographs and pictures by Sunday painters, a couple of which feature colourful local boatsheds.

The pleasant Californian puts me in his chair, clips my horny toenails with a practised hand (that he relishes his work is obvious), and then applies a scalpel to the callous on the ball of my right foot. And oh but what a whittler the good doctor is, an ace excisor of tough but superfluous tissues.

'And now for the Big Reveal,' he says. 'If your metatarsal is to mend itself, it's going to need the support of a sturdy platform, and this fine appliance will give you that while also sparing you the encumbrance of crutches.' And he fits me with a something that's not quite a moonboot, a something somewhere between sandal and lacerated galosh, all matt-black Velcro straps and thick black sole: the Post-Op Shoe manufactured by Bird & Cronin of Eagan, Minnesota.

AMBUSHING MYSELF

1

Of course, the broken metatarsal in my foot turns out *not* to be a broken metatarsal. What the broken metatarsal turns out to be is the onset of arthritis. (This is Dr Halpine's latest diagnosis. As to my attractive post-op shoe, he suggests that I stick to it 'for the time being'.)

2

Sunday. I'm walking down Marion St minding my own business when I come a tremendous gutser.

Bollocks. Buggeration. Thank you, God. And then the shock kicks in, entraining fire and ice.

No, but really, this was something else. I felt as if I'd been fired from a cannon into the asphalt surface of the footpath.

A sensible young woman helped me to my feet, but I didn't much care for being on my feet and sat back down again. Sat back down and marvelled at my state for many, many minutes.

3

Later, at home, when at last I realized that I could barely use my left arm and was losing articulation in my right knee, I called an ambulance. Which took me (none too swiftly) to A&E, where I spent the next three hours listening to a baby being tortured in the cubicle next to mine. (There's always a baby being tortured.)

THE TATTOOED MAN

There's little unmarked skin on his hands, his arms, his
face.

He's been tagged by many uncouth hands, extensively
scribbled on, talentlessly pricked and inked all over.

It's as if he's wearing a grey body stocking. It's as if
he's been rolled in the warm grey ashes of unholy fires.

Easy to feel affronted. Easy to feel a prim disapproval.
But then it dawns on me that this outrageous fright is
really as white and skinny as myself (though forty years
younger). And when I'm told that he's deaf and dumb
and a product of 'state care' (boys' homes, borstals, jails),
I begin to understand how he came to be so grimly
decorated.

Coca-Cola.
Western Union.
The Gaboon viper.

A dead child's shoe.
Computerized axial tomography.
The lifetime of a fact.

Debussy's velvet revolution.
America's aversion to atheists.
A wettish day with lots of English mist.

A bottle full of smoke.
A clockwork conundrum.
A blue swatch torn from an afternoon in Rome.

GOING TO THE PICTURES,
WAY BACK WHEN

South Pacific
The Ten Commandments

Terence Stamp in *Billy Budd*
Robert Preston in *The Music Man*

West Side Story
The Guns of Navarone
The Bridge on the River Kwai

But then came *Dr No* and Old Spice –
Dr No and Old Spice and Peter Stuyvesant cigarettes

PENIS-ENVY *CIRCA* 1970

Odours of beer and Jeyes fluid.
The startling girth of John Girvan's cock.

REMEMBERING JOHN'S SUICIDE
BY SHOTGUN

Blood on the tracks, suddenly

Blood on the tracks
and blood in the trees

KINGSBEER & CO

i

My handwriting this morning suggests
a chimp's knitting.

ii

Osteoarthritis = wear and tear.
Which I'm trying to feel I've earned,
richly deserve.

iii

I talk to a man who tells me
that his favourite painter is Canaletto.

All very well and good, yes, but *surely* . . .

iv

Jeff Kingsbeer and Mark Hopko,
Mitch Silver and George Ashkettle
(names I've been collecting;
names I've snaffled, pocketed adroitly) –

they'll all go into the novel I'll never write,
the novel I'm not writing, even now.

SUMMER

1

Morning, and I'm doing what I do,
playing with a few silly words,
fiddling with a few flaccid lines.

2

Sunshine in the kitchen. Loads
of it. A hot opportunity
to defrost the fridge

(my cute, cuboidal midget of a fridge).

3

I'm no longer opting
for *big* reads. Am not about to try
Sabbath's Theatre for the umpteenth time.

4

I like what's slim.
I like what's portable.
I look to what I've read before with pleasure.

Barthelme's *Paradise*, for instance –
a zestful wee caprice as light as cake.

5

Or John Berger's *Photocopies*.
Or Nicholson Baker's *Box of Matches*.
Or George Saunders' *Pastoralia*.

6

What was the city like, in my drinking days?
Was it really as sunny as memory suggests?
Was it really as cold and wet
as I seem to remember it being?

7

Dear Ashleigh,

Please forgive me –
I open my mouth and dreadful things
totter out of it.

8

The 1970s. Modernity!

My new typewriter had
a shallow, wedgy shape,
a profile like that of a Maserati.

(Marijuana was popular,
semi-religiously so,
but I was some sort of throwback,
a sly retard determined to drink
the skull-and-crossbones plonk,
the purple turpentine.)

SOME QUESTIONS IT AMUSED ME
TO ANSWER

Who is your favourite literary character?

Lionel Asbo.

**What was the first book you read
from cover to cover?**

Treasure Island. I think.

**You're planning a literary dinner party.
Which three writers do you invite?**

Laurence Sterne, Donald Barthelme and Wendy Cope.
And I serve them savoury mince and poached eggs
on toast, about which Don has many good-natured,
food-savvy queries.

SHOOT

Insulin and Weet-Bix for breakfast. Three Weet-Bix with a teaspoon of sugar. And I sit here perking like an old Cona coffee percolator.

*

I don't know where they go, my incoming texts. They arrive in my phone, ding-dong, but I can't locate the limbo into which they're dropped.

I've almost given up on this new device of mine, a 'better' mousetrap designed by a bunch of nine-year-olds. But it's *not* a better mousetrap, it's the worst mousetrap ever, a maze of misdirections and meaningless graphics – and resolutely unintuitive.

*

Suddenly I'm 68, it seems. Just as I was suddenly 65.

Late last year, I conducted a short-lived experiment in Not Writing. It didn't make me totally unhappy, but I missed my daily stint at the coalface. I don't want to waffle on and on, producing ever weaker, paler stuff, but nor do I want to shut up shop completely.

*

The *clitch* and *clatch* of her quiet Minolta. Blue and black the mirror of her lens. She's going for a day-for-night effect, but does she have the know-how?

I don my beanie, try to measure up – she wants me poor and priestly in my own shabby coat. (Should I mention my flu, my problematic foot?)

Be*hind* me is where she wants to be; I can feel her firing rays at my dorsal surface. (Not far from here is the Elephant House, the elephant's puce pong, the big bold pong of elephant entire. And in this very street there used to live a bust of Bertrand Russell.)

GROWING UP IN TAMAR ST

The matt-black innards of my father's Kodak.
My snapshot of the bison at the zoo.

MY FATHER'S TOOLS

Spokeshave, tinsnips, ancient cobbler's last.
(You'll often find me
under the house like this.)

LOSING MY WHISTLE

'Shite and onions!'

*

This is the way it is, these days:
when I look in the mirror, I see my grandfather.

*

I discovered recently that I can no longer whistle.
The muscles in my cheeks have forgotten how,
can no longer form the necessary embouchure.

(Am I also beginning to lose
my appetite for words,
for reading and writing, both?)

Sam's a smart young bloke working at New World, and he tells me that he wants to join the police force.

Is he tall enough to qualify for training? And won't police work brutalize the kid? I keep my reservations to myself, but feel obliged to offer encouragement. 'You'll sail through your interview,' I say. 'If I were screening you, I'd snap you up – I can see a big future for you as a detective.'

I remember being processed by one particular cop. A *droll* character. He photographed and fingerprinted me, then stood me up against a rule that measured my height. 'You're five feet nine and a half,' he remarked. 'Too short to be a policeman.'

This was in the cells at Central, yes. Long ago, in the days of my drinking, yes. I was always pissed and always getting pinched; I weighed perhaps ten stone wringing wet, and the fuzz would see me coming and make an easy arrest.

The days of wine and roses, as it were. And I weaved my way from pub to pub without anyone ever laying a finger on me. Anyone other than cops, that is.

CHOSEN

I'm sitting outside the Victoria St Café (coffee, cigarette, my usual table) when a passing dog stops at my feet and gazes up at me with bright black eyes.

'He wants to say hello,' his mistress tells me. 'Would you mind terribly?'

'Not at all,' I say, and give the soulful pooch a gentle roughing-up.

'He does this,' says the woman.

'?'

'Each and every day, at some point on our walk, he stops and lets me know that this is today's person, the party he wants to be introduced to.'

SUNDRIES

The blue doom of summer.

*

A baby sneezes, *splitch!*

*

White plastic chairs.
Those moulded plastic chairs produced
by some huge factory in China?

Nicholson Baker has one, and so do I,
but Baker takes his chair to the creek
and treats it to other little outings
while mine never gets to leave the house.

*

Tagline of the new Lego movie: *They come in pieces.*

Only in the quietest moments
does it make itself heard,
atomically sublime and self-sustaining:

the ping of my own existence,
ping of my own existence,
ping of my own continuing existence.

THE SONG THRUSH AND ME

i

A throstle in a downpour.
A throstle on a post in heavy rain,

singing his heart out
(big heart, big voice, big song).

ii

Pernicious anaemia.
This is the weird complaint

my doctor has added
to my suite of diseases –

I've been given a Victorian disorder,
a steampunk malady
(it even *sounds* archaic and defunct).

TALKING TO MYSELF (AGAIN)

'We seem to be remembering a windless 3:00 a.m.'

'A moonless 3:00 a.m. long ago.'

'We'd walked down from some high place in Roseneath. Reached the band rotunda on Oriental Parade. And that was when a plenitude of snow began to fall.'

'A rare event.'

'Had we been to one of Auton Lowe's film evenings?'

'He'd screened Jean Cocteau's *Orphée*. A work of surprising technical excellence.'

'We were struck particularly by its special effects, some as old as cinema itself but born again, refreshed and repurposed.'

'And here was yet another special effect: a sibilance of silly, silent snow.'

IAN

I still see Ian Lee from time to time.
A dilapidated version, mind you.
A fucked-up version of the sweet young man
I knew in the 1980s.

Sepia teeth.
Beard like I don't know what.
Long black poacher's coat.
And on the methadone-maintenance programme
to this day.

I liked him way back when
and I like him still.
He gets his daily fix from the chemist,
buys his few groceries at Countdown,
retreats to his tidy council flat.

A brave fragility, his.
Or so I've always thought.

IRRATIONALITY

I don't fear death, but I *do* fear cremation.

ADDENDA

'Ancient of Days, old friend, no one believes you'll come back.' Charles Wright

'Beneath the pieties of art lie the brutalities of talent. It really *is* all in how good you potchke up the paint.' Adam Gopnik

'Strange, how dirty the attempt to speak seriously made him feel.' John Updike

'I drank a lot, I lost my job,
I lived like nothing mattered.
Then you stopped, and came across
my little bridge of fallen answers.' Leonard Cohen

'. . . I feel the sun warming up the clear flamingos that swim around in my eyeballs.' Nicholson Baker

'The earth is blue, like an orange.' Tristan Tzara

'. . . the neon strips came on with a flustered whinny.' Martin Amis

'Several of the male members of his family had lived to be fifty-nine or sixty. "Grow or die" was the maxim that most accorded with his experience and when he did not think of himself as a giraffe he thought of himself as a tree, a palm, schematically a skinny curving vertical with a lot of furor at the top.' Donald Barthelme

Screenwriter Terry Southern's last words: 'What's the hold-up?'